EMMANUEL JOSEPH

The Symphony of Survival, Blending Art, Psychology, and Ecology for a Sustainable Future

Contents

1

Chapter 1: The Prelude of Existence

Our journey begins in a world pulsating with life, where every element harmonizes to create a symphony of survival. The natural environment, humanity, and the arts intertwine to form the basis of this profound narrative. We explore how primitive humans relied on their surroundings for survival, crafting tools and art from the materials available to them. Through the ages, these creative expressions evolved, revealing a deep connection between our species and the ecosystems we inhabit.

In the beginning, life on Earth existed in a state of delicate balance. Every organism, from the tiniest microorganism to the largest predator, played a vital role in maintaining the harmony of the natural world. This intricate web of life, often referred to as the "circle of life," ensured that ecosystems remained healthy and vibrant. As humans emerged and evolved, they became an integral part of this symphony, relying on nature for sustenance, shelter, and inspiration.

Early human societies were deeply connected to their environments. They crafted tools from stones, bones, and wood, using their surroundings to create everything they needed for survival. Art, too, played a crucial role in these ancient communities. Cave paintings, carvings, and sculptures were not merely decorative; they served as vital means of communication, storytelling, and preserving cultural knowledge. These early artworks offer glimpses into the minds of our ancestors, revealing their reverence for the natural world.

As civilizations grew, so did the complexity of their artistic expressions. Ancient Egyptians adorned their temples and tombs with intricate hieroglyphs and frescoes, while the Greeks and Romans created sculptures and mosaics that celebrated the beauty of nature and human achievement. Throughout history, art has served as a mirror, reflecting humanity's evolving relationship with the environment. The artistic endeavors of these early cultures highlight the profound interconnectedness between humans and nature.

Psychologically, creative expression has always provided humans with a means to process their experiences, express emotions, and connect with others. This evolutionary advantage allowed our ancestors to form strong social bonds and navigate the challenges of survival. Art, in its many forms, has served as a universal language, transcending barriers of time and culture. The psychological benefits of creative expression continue to be relevant today, offering insights into our intrinsic connection to the natural world.

Paragraph 5

Imagine a prehistoric tribe living in a lush valley, surrounded by dense forests and meandering rivers. One day, a member of the tribe discovers a series of strange tracks leading toward a hidden cave. Intrigued, the tribe ventures inside and finds a breathtaking display of cave paintings depicting the migration patterns of local wildlife. These artworks provide crucial information about the seasonal movements of animals, helping the tribe plan their hunting and gathering activities. Through their art, the tribe ensures their survival, passing down vital knowledge to future generations.

2

Chapter 2: Art as a Mirror of Nature

Art has always been a reflection of the natural world, capturing its beauty, mysteries, and raw power. This chapter delves into the relationship between art and nature, examining how artists have drawn inspiration from their surroundings to create masterpieces that resonate with the human spirit. From cave paintings to contemporary environmental art, we explore how artistic expression has evolved alongside our understanding of the environment.

Prehistoric cave art offers a fascinating glimpse into the minds of our ancient ancestors. These early artists meticulously depicted scenes of hunting, dancing, and everyday life on the walls of caves. The images of animals, people, and abstract symbols reveal a deep connection to the natural world. These artworks were not just representations; they were believed to hold spiritual significance, serving as a bridge between the human and the divine.

As human societies developed, so did their artistic expressions. The classical art of ancient Greece and Rome showcased a deep appreciation for the natural world. Renowned painters like Leonardo da Vinci and Vincent van Gogh drew inspiration from their surroundings, capturing the beauty of landscapes, flora, and fauna. Their works continue to resonate with audiences today, reminding us of the enduring power of nature to inspire creativity and wonder.

In the modern era, environmental art movements have emerged, seeking to raise awareness about ecological issues and advocate for conservation. Artists like Andy Goldsworthy and Christo & Jeanne-Claude create temporary installations that highlight the fragility and impermanence of the natural world. Through their art, they invite viewers to contemplate their relationship with the environment and consider the impact of human activities on the planet.

Psychologically, nature-inspired art can have profound effects on individuals and communities. Studies have shown that exposure to natural environments and artwork depicting nature can reduce stress, improve mood, and enhance overall well-being. Art therapy, which often incorporates nature elements, has been used to help individuals cope with trauma, anxiety, and other mental health challenges. The therapeutic power of nature-inspired art underscores the deep connection between the human psyche and the natural world.

Paragraph 5

Consider the story of an artist named Maya, who grew up in a bustling urban environment. Feeling disconnected from nature, she began to explore nearby parks and natural areas, drawing inspiration from the landscapes she encountered. Maya's art evolved to incorporate natural materials like leaves, branches, and stones, creating intricate sculptures that celebrated the beauty of the environment. Through her work, Maya not only found a sense of peace and fulfillment but also inspired others to appreciate and protect the natural world.

3

Chapter 3: The Psychological Symphony

The human mind is a complex and intricate orchestra, with each psychological component playing a vital role in our perception of the world. This chapter explores the connections between psychology, art, and ecology, revealing how our mental states influence our interactions with the environment. We delve into the concepts of eco-psychology and biophilia, examining how our innate love for nature shapes our behaviors and attitudes.

Eco-psychology is a field that examines the relationship between human beings and the natural world, emphasizing the psychological benefits of connecting with nature. Biophilia, a related concept, suggests that humans have an inherent affinity for the natural world. These ideas have gained traction in recent years, as researchers and practitioners recognize the importance of fostering a deep connection with nature for mental and emotional well-being.

Spending time in nature has been shown to have numerous psychological benefits, including reduced stress, improved mood, and enhanced cognitive function. Engaging in creative activities, such as drawing, painting, or crafting, can further amplify these benefits. By combining art and nature, individuals can experience a heightened sense of well-being and a deeper appreciation for the environment.

Art therapy, which utilizes creative expression as a means of healing, has been found to be particularly effective in promoting mental well-being and fostering a connection with the natural world. Incorporating nature elements into art therapy sessions can help individuals process their emotions, develop coping strategies, and build resilience. This holistic approach highlights the interconnectedness of art, psychology, and ecology in promoting overall health and well-being.

Environmental degradation can have profound effects on mental health, contributing to feelings of anxiety, depression, and helplessness. Recognizing the importance of ecological conservation is essential for maintaining both the health of the planet and the well-being of its inhabitants. By fostering a sense of stewardship and responsibility for the environment, individuals can contribute to a healthier, more sustainable world.

Paragraph 5

Imagine the story of Alex, a young person struggling with anxiety and depression. Feeling overwhelmed by the demands of daily life, Alex discovers a small community garden in their neighborhood. Drawn to the tranquility of the space, they begin to spend time there, tending to the plants and creating art inspired by the natural surroundings. Through this connection with nature and creative expression, Alex experiences a renewed sense of purpose and emotional healing, demonstrating the profound impact of eco-psychology and biophilia.

4

Chapter 4: The Harmony of Ecosystems

Ecosystems are delicate and interdependent networks, each component playing a crucial role in maintaining balance. This chapter examines the intricate relationships within ecosystems, highlighting the importance of biodiversity and the consequences of disrupting these natural harmonies. We explore how art and psychology can contribute to ecological understanding and conservation efforts.

Ecosystems are complex networks of living organisms and their physical environments, working together to maintain balance and sustain life. Each component, from plants and animals to microorganisms and abiotic factors, plays a vital role in the overall health of the ecosystem. Understanding these intricate relationships is essential for appreciating the interconnectedness of all living things.

Biodiversity, the variety of life forms within an ecosystem, is crucial for maintaining ecological balance. Each species, whether it be a keystone predator or a tiny pollinator, contributes to the stability and resilience of the ecosystem. The loss of biodiversity can have cascading effects, disrupting the delicate balance and leading to ecological collapse. Conserving biodiversity is essential for ensuring the long-term health and sustainability of our planet.

Human activities, such as deforestation, pollution, and climate change, have significant impacts on ecosystems worldwide. These actions can lead to habitat loss, species extinction, and the degradation of natural resources. Recognizing the importance of sustainable practices is crucial for mitigating these impacts and protecting the health of our ecosystems.

Art and psychology can play a significant role in fostering environmental awareness and conservation efforts. Through creative expression, individuals can develop a deeper understanding of ecological principles and the importance of biodiversity. Art can serve as a powerful tool for advocacy, inspiring people to take action and make positive changes in their communities.

Paragraph 5

Consider the story of a coastal community facing the threat of a declining marine ecosystem due to pollution and overfishing. Inspired by their love for the ocean, local artists and psychologists collaborate to create an immersive art installation that

continue

Certainly! Let's continue with the writing:

Chapter 4: The Harmony of Ecosystems (cont.)

Paragraph 5
Consider the story of a coastal community facing the threat of a declining marine ecosystem due to pollution and overfishing. Inspired by their love for the ocean, local artists and psychologists collaborate to create an immersive art installation that showcases the beauty and fragility of marine life. Through this powerful visual experience, they raise awareness about the importance of conservation and inspire the community to take collective action to protect their coastal environment.

6

Chapter 5: The Dance of Adaptation

Adaptation is a fundamental aspect of survival, allowing species to thrive in ever-changing environments. This chapter explores the concept of adaptation in nature, art, and human behavior. We examine how creative expression can facilitate adaptation, both on an individual and societal level, and how ecological principles can inspire innovative solutions to contemporary challenges.

Adaptation is the process by which organisms adjust to changes in their environment, enhancing their chances of survival and reproduction. In the natural world, this can take many forms, from physical changes in an organism's anatomy to behavioral modifications that improve its ability to find food or avoid predators. Understanding the mechanisms of adaptation provides valuable insights into the resilience and ingenuity of life on Earth.

Examples of remarkable adaptations can be found across the animal kingdom. The chameleon, for instance, has developed the ability to change its skin color to blend in with its surroundings, avoiding detection by predators. Similarly, the arctic fox's fur changes color with the seasons, providing camouflage in both snowy and tundra environments. These adaptations highlight the incredible diversity of strategies that organisms employ to navigate their ever-changing habitats.

In human society, creativity and art play a crucial role in adaptation and problem-solving. Creative expression allows individuals to explore new ideas, communicate complex concepts, and develop innovative solutions to challenges. Whether through visual art, music, or literature, creativity fosters flexibility and resilience, enabling people to adapt to changing circumstances and overcome obstacles.

Ecological principles can inspire innovative solutions to contemporary challenges, such as climate change and resource scarcity. By observing how natural systems function and adapt, humans can develop sustainable practices that mimic these processes. This approach, known as biomimicry, has led to advancements in fields such as architecture, agriculture, and technology, promoting harmony between human activities and the natural world.

Paragraph 5

Imagine the story of an artist named Sarah, who lives in a coastal city facing the threat of rising sea levels due to climate change. Inspired by the resilience of local marine life, Sarah creates a series of sculptures that mimic the adaptive strategies of these organisms. Her work not only raises awareness about the impact of climate change but also inspires the community to implement innovative solutions, such as building resilient infrastructure and adopting sustainable practices.

7

Chapter 6: The Rhythm of Resilience

Resilience is the ability to withstand and recover from adversity. This chapter delves into the concept of resilience in nature, art, and human psychology. We explore how ecosystems and individuals demonstrate resilience in the face of challenges, and how creative expression can foster a sense of hope and strength.

Resilience in nature is exemplified by ecosystems' ability to recover from disturbances, such as natural disasters or human activities. This adaptive capacity is often supported by biodiversity, which provides a variety of species and genetic diversity that can contribute to ecosystem recovery. Understanding the factors that promote ecological resilience is essential for developing conservation strategies that support the health and stability of natural systems.

The psychological concept of resilience refers to an individual's ability to cope with stress, adversity, and trauma. Resilient individuals can navigate challenges, adapt to changing circumstances, and maintain a sense of well-being. Factors that contribute to psychological resilience include social support, positive coping strategies, and a sense of purpose and meaning in life.

Art plays a significant role in promoting resilience by providing a means of expression, reflection, and healing. Creative activities can help individuals process difficult emotions, develop coping strategies, and build a sense of hope and strength. Art therapy, in particular, has been found to be effective in supporting individuals who have experienced trauma, loss, or other significant challenges.

The resilience of ecosystems is closely tied to the concept of ecological restoration, which involves the process of assisting the recovery of degraded, damaged, or destroyed ecosystems. Restoration efforts can include reforestation, wetland rehabilitation, and the reintroduction of native species. These initiatives contribute to the overall health and stability of ecosystems, promoting resilience in the face of ongoing environmental changes.

Paragraph 5

Consider the story of a community affected by a devastating wildfire that destroys homes and natural habitats. In the aftermath of the disaster, local artists and psychologists come together to create a public art project that helps the community process their grief and rebuild their sense of hope. Through workshops and collaborative art installations, residents find strength and resilience, demonstrating the power of creative expression in fostering recovery and renewal.

8

Chapter 7: The Melody of Mindfulness

Mindfulness is a practice that encourages individuals to be present and fully engaged in the moment. This chapter explores the connections between mindfulness, art, and ecology, revealing how these practices can enhance our understanding of the natural world and promote sustainable living. We examine the psychological benefits of mindfulness and how creative expression can facilitate a deeper connection with the environment.

Mindfulness is the practice of cultivating awareness and acceptance of the present moment. By focusing on the here and now, individuals can develop a greater sense of clarity, calm, and well-being. Mindfulness has been shown to reduce stress, improve mental health, and enhance overall quality of life. This practice encourages individuals to engage fully with their surroundings, fostering a deeper appreciation for the natural world.

Integrating mindfulness into artistic expression can enhance the creative process and promote a sense of connection with the environment. Practices such as mindful drawing, painting, or sculpting encourage individuals to observe their surroundings closely, capturing the intricate details and beauty of the natural world. This heightened awareness can lead to a deeper understanding of ecological principles and a greater appreciation for the interconnectedness of all living things.

Nature-based mindfulness practices, such as forest bathing or eco-meditation, offer opportunities to connect with the environment in meaningful ways. These practices involve immersing oneself in natural settings, engaging the senses, and observing the sights, sounds, and sensations of the surroundings. By fostering a sense of presence and awareness, nature-based mindfulness can enhance mental well-being and promote a deeper connection with the environment.

Mindful living extends beyond individual practices to encompass sustainable behaviors and ecological stewardship. By cultivating mindfulness in daily life, individuals can develop a greater awareness of their impact on the environment and make conscious choices that support sustainability. This holistic approach encourages a harmonious relationship with the natural world, promoting both personal well-being and ecological health.

Paragraph 5

Imagine the story of an individual named David, who feels overwhelmed by the demands of modern life. Seeking solace, David begins to practice mindfulness through nature walks and sketching the landscapes he encounters. As he becomes more attuned to the natural world, David develops a deep appreciation for the environment and adopts sustainable practices in his daily life. Through mindfulness and creative expression, David finds a sense of peace and purpose, illustrating the transformative power of these practices.

9

Chapter 8: The Chords of Community

Communities are the backbone of human society, providing support, connection, and a sense of belonging. This chapter explores the importance of community in fostering sustainability and resilience. We examine how art and psychology can strengthen community bonds and promote collective action for environmental conservation.

Communities play a vital role in shaping the social and environmental landscape. They provide a sense of belonging, support, and shared identity, fostering connections that contribute to individual and collective well-being. Strong communities are essential for promoting social cohesion, resilience, and sustainable development.

Art has the power to build and strengthen community connections, serving as a medium for shared expression, celebration, and reflection. Public art projects, community murals, and collaborative performances can bring people together, creating opportunities for dialogue, understanding, and collective action. These creative endeavors can also raise awareness about environmental issues, inspiring communities to work together toward common goals.

The psychological benefits of belonging to a supportive and engaged community are well-documented. Individuals who feel connected to their communities experience greater mental and emotional well-being, lower levels of stress, and a stronger sense of purpose. Community involvement also provides opportunities for personal growth, skill development, and meaningful contributions to society.

Community-led environmental conservation initiatives are essential for addressing local and global ecological challenges. By working together, communities can develop and implement sustainable practices, restore natural habitats, and advocate for environmental policies. These collective efforts contribute to the health and resilience of both human and natural systems, promoting a sustainable future for all.

Paragraph 5

Consider the story of a small town that faces the threat of a polluted river, endangering the health of its residents and local wildlife. Inspired by their love for their community and the environment, local artists, psychologists, and activists come together to organize a river cleanup event. Through art installations, educational workshops, and community gatherings, they raise awareness about the importance of water conservation and inspire residents to take action. Their collective efforts lead to the restoration of the river, demonstrating the power of community in fostering environmental stewardship.

10

Chapter 9: The Crescendo of Creativity

Creativity is a powerful force that drives innovation, problem-solving, and personal growth. This chapter explores the role of creativity in art, psychology, and ecology, revealing how creative expression can inspire positive change and foster a sustainable future. We examine the connections between creativity and ecological thinking, and how artistic endeavors can promote environmental awareness and conservation.

Creativity is an essential aspect of human life, enabling individuals to explore new ideas, solve problems, and express themselves in unique ways. It is a driving force behind artistic expression, scientific discovery, and technological advancement. By nurturing creativity, individuals can develop the skills and perspectives needed to navigate the complexities of the modern world and contribute to a more sustainable future.

Artistic expression is a powerful manifestation of creativity, allowing individuals to convey their thoughts, emotions, and experiences through various mediums. The process of creating art can be deeply therapeutic, providing a means of coping with stress, processing emotions, and finding a sense of purpose. Additionally, art can serve as a catalyst for social change, raising awareness about important issues and inspiring collective action.

The connections between creativity and ecological thinking are evident in the principles of biomimicry, which involves drawing inspiration from nature to develop innovative solutions to human challenges. By observing and emulating the adaptive strategies of plants, animals, and ecosystems, humans can create sustainable technologies, designs, and practices that harmonize with the natural world. This approach fosters a deep appreciation for the ingenuity of nature and promotes environmental stewardship.

Creative projects can play a significant role in promoting environmental awareness and conservation. Art installations, public performances, and community workshops can engage audiences, spark conversations, and inspire action. By highlighting the beauty and fragility of the natural world, these projects can encourage individuals and communities to adopt sustainable practices and advocate for environmental protection.

Paragraph 5

Consider the story of an artist named Emma, who is passionate about marine conservation. She creates a series of sculptures using recycled materials, depicting the vibrant and diverse life forms found in the ocean. Through her art, Emma raises awareness about the impact of plastic pollution on marine ecosystems and inspires her community to reduce their use of single-use plastics. Her creative efforts not only highlight the importance of environmental conservation but also demonstrate the potential of art to drive positive change.

11

Chapter 10: The Symphony of Sustainability

Sustainability is the key to ensuring the long-term health and well-being of our planet and its inhabitants. This chapter explores the principles of sustainability and how they can be integrated into art, psychology, and daily life. We examine the role of creative expression in promoting sustainable practices and how individuals and communities can contribute to a more sustainable future.

Sustainability is a holistic approach to living that seeks to balance the needs of the present with the ability of future generations to meet their own needs. It encompasses environmental, social, and economic dimensions, emphasizing the importance of conservation, equity, and responsible resource management. By adopting sustainable practices, individuals and communities can contribute to the health and resilience of the planet.

Art and creativity can play a significant role in promoting sustainable practices and raising awareness about environmental issues. Through visual art, music, literature, and performance, artists can convey powerful messages about the importance of conservation, the impact of human activities on the environment, and the need for collective action. Creative projects can engage diverse audiences, fostering a sense of shared responsibility and inspiring positive change.

The psychological benefits of adopting sustainable behaviors are well-documented. Individuals who engage in eco-friendly practices often experience a greater sense of purpose, well-being, and connection to the natural world. Mindfulness and intentionality in daily life can also promote sustainable living, encouraging individuals to make conscious choices that support environmental health and social equity.

Collective action and community involvement are essential for achieving sustainability goals. By working together, communities can develop and implement strategies that promote environmental conservation, social justice, and economic resilience. Collaborative initiatives, such as community gardens, renewable energy projects, and conservation programs, can have a significant impact on local and global sustainability efforts.

Paragraph 5

Imagine the story of a young activist named Amina, who is passionate about creating a more sustainable future. She organizes a series of community events that combine art, education, and hands-on activities to raise awareness about environmental issues and promote sustainable practices. Through her efforts, Amina inspires her community to adopt eco-friendly behaviors, demonstrating the power of creativity and collective action in driving positive change.

12

Chapter 11: The Overture of Optimism

Optimism is a powerful mindset that can inspire hope, resilience, and positive action. This chapter explores the connections between optimism, art, psychology, and ecology, revealing how a positive outlook can drive meaningful change. We examine the role of creative expression in fostering optimism and how it can contribute to a sustainable and thriving future.

Optimism is the belief that positive outcomes are possible, even in the face of challenges and adversity. This mindset can have profound effects on mental and emotional well-being, fostering resilience, motivation, and a sense of purpose. Optimism encourages individuals to view setbacks as opportunities for growth and to approach problems with a solution-oriented attitude.

Art and creativity can play a significant role in promoting optimism and inspiring hope. Through their work, artists can convey messages of resilience, possibility, and positive change. Creative expression allows individuals to envision a better future, explore new ideas, and communicate their dreams and aspirations. Art can serve as a powerful tool for fostering a sense of hope and collective action.

The connections between optimism and ecological thinking are evident in the principles of sustainability and conservation. By adopting an optimistic out-look, individuals and communities can approach environmental challenges with a sense of possibility and determination. This mindset encourages proactive efforts to protect the environment, restore natural habitats, and develop innovative solutions to ecological issues.

Cultivating optimism can also have positive effects on mental health and well-being. Individuals who maintain a positive outlook are more likely to experience greater happiness, reduced stress, and improved overall quality of life. Optimism can also foster a sense of connection and solidarity, encouraging individuals to work together toward common goals and create a more just and sustainable world.

Paragraph 5

Consider the story of a community facing the challenges of climate change and environmental degradation. Despite the difficulties, local artists and ac-tivists come together to create a public art project that envisions a sustainable and thriving future. Through murals, sculptures, and performances, they convey messages of hope, resilience, and possibility. Their work inspires the community to take positive action, demonstrating the transformative power of optimism and creativity.

13

Chapter 12: The Finale of Harmony

As we conclude our journey, we reflect on the interconnectedness of art, psychology, and ecology, and the importance of harmony in ensuring the survival and well-being of all living beings. This chapter highlights the key themes explored throughout the book and offers practical insights for integrating these principles into daily life. We emphasize the power of creative expression in fostering a sustainable future and the role of individuals and communities in driving positive change.

The interconnectedness of art, psychology, and ecology is a central theme that underscores the importance of harmony in our lives. By recognizing and nurturing these connections, individuals and communities can develop a deeper understanding of themselves, their environment, and their place in the world. This holistic approach fosters a sense of balance, well-being, and sustainability.

Throughout this book, we have explored the various ways in which art, psychology, and ecology intersect to promote a sustainable and thriving future. From the psychological benefits of creative expression to the ecological principles of adaptation and resilience, these themes offer valuable insights for navigating the complexities of modern life and contributing to the health of the planet.

Creative expression plays a pivotal role in fostering environmental awareness, promoting sustainable practices, and inspiring positive change. By engaging with art and creativity, individuals can develop a deeper connection to the natural world and a greater sense of responsibility for its well-being. Artistic endeavors can also serve as powerful tools for advocacy, education, and community building.

Collective action is essential for achieving sustainability goals and ensuring the long-term health and well-being of our planet. By working together, individuals and communities can develop and implement strategies that promote conservation, equity, and resilience. Collaboration and shared responsibility are key to addressing the complex challenges of our time and creating a more just and sustainable world.

Paragraph 5

As we conclude our journey, let us reflect on the power of harmony and the potential for positive change. By embracing the interconnectedness of art, psychology, and ecology, we can cultivate a deeper appreciation for the natural world and our place within it. Through creative expression, mindfulness, and collective action, we can contribute to a sustainable and thriving future for all living beings.

"The Symphony of Survival: Blending Art, Psychology, and Ecology for a Sustainable Future":

In a world teeming with life, the threads of art, psychology, and ecology weave together to form an intricate tapestry of survival. "The Symphony of Survival: Blending Art, Psychology, and Ecology for a Sustainable Future" takes readers on a captivating journey through time and nature, exploring how these interconnected disciplines shape our existence and inspire us to create a more sustainable future.

From the dawn of human history, art has served as a mirror to the natural world, capturing its beauty, mysteries, and raw power. This book delves into the evolution of artistic expression, from ancient cave paintings to modern environmental art, revealing the profound connection between humanity and the environment. Through engaging stories and historical insights, readers will discover how art has influenced our understanding of nature and our role within it.

The psychological components of our minds play a crucial role in how we perceive and interact with the world around us. By exploring the concepts of eco-psychology and biophilia, "The Symphony of Survival" reveals the innate love humans have for nature and the mental health benefits of connecting with the environment. Through personal anecdotes and scientific research, readers will gain a deeper appreciation for the psychological symphony that shapes our behaviors and attitudes.

Ecosystems are delicate and interdependent networks, each component playing a vital role in maintaining balance. This book examines the intricate relationships within ecosystems, highlighting the importance of biodiversity and the consequences of disrupting these natural harmonies. Through compelling stories of communities coming together to restore damaged ecosystems, readers will learn how art and psychology can contribute to ecological understanding and conservation efforts.

Adaptation and resilience are fundamental aspects of survival, allowing species to thrive in ever-changing environments. "The Symphony of Survival" explores how creative expression can facilitate adaptation, both on an individual and societal level, and how ecological principles can inspire innovative solutions to contemporary challenges. By blending art, psychology, and ecology, this book offers a holistic approach to navigating the complexities of modern life and fostering a sustainable future.

As we journey through the pages of "The Symphony of Survival," readers will be inspired by the harmonious interplay of art, psychology, and ecology. The book emphasizes the power of creative expression in promoting environmental awareness, resilience, and sustainable practices. By embracing these interconnected principles, we can contribute to a thriving and harmonious world for future generations.